Anonymous

Sabbath Bells Chimed by the Poets

Anonymous

Sabbath Bells Chimed by the Poets

ISBN/EAN: 9783743350267

Manufactured in Europe, USA, Canada, Australia, Japa

Cover: Foto ©ninafisch / pixelio.de

Manufactured and distributed by brebook publishing software (www.brebook.com)

Anonymous

Sabbath Bells Chimed by the Poets

SABBATH BELLS

CHIMED BY THE POETS.

CHIMED

By the Poets.

"Sundays observe: think when the Bells do chime,
T.s Angels' music."—GEORGE HERBERT.

ELEGANTLY ILLUSTRATED.

PHILADELPHIA:
PUBLISHED BY E. H. BUTLER & CO.
1870.

Entered, according to Act of Congress, in the year 1856, by
E. H. BUTLER & CO.,
In the Clerk's Office of the District Court for the Eastern District of Pennsylvania.

Contents.

		PAGE
THE SABBATH,	GRAHAME,	17
SUNDAY,	HERBERT,	20
SABBATH MORNING,	SIGOURNEY,	23
A SPRING SABBATH WALK,	GRAHAME,	24
THE HOUSE OF GOD,	BP. MANT,	25
ENGLISH CHURCHES,	L. E. LANDON,	26
'TIS SWEET TO HEAR A BROOK,	COLERIDGE,	28
A CHURCHYARD SCENE,	JOHN WILSON,	28
A SUMMER SABBATH WALK,	GRAHAME,	31
THE VILLAGE CHURCH,	ROGERS,	33
THE SABBATH,	WM. HOWITT,	33
SUNDAY WALKS,	CLARE,	35
THE SABBATH,	SIR E. B. LYTTON,	42
THE SABBATH,	CUNNINGHAM,	43
THE CHURCHYARD,	MISS BOWLES,	45
THE VILLAGE CHURCH,	BP. MANT,	48
THEY PURSUE THE PEBBLY WALK,	HOOD,	49
THE CHURCH BELLS,	BP. MANT,	50

CONTENTS.

		PAGE
AN AUTUMN SABBATH WALK,	GRAHAME,	51
SABBATH DAYS,	BARTON,	52
HOW SOFT THE MUSIC, ETC.,	COWPER,	54
THE BELL,	SOUTHEY,	54
THE VILLAGE CHURCH,	ANON.,	55
THE DAY OF REST,	GRINFIELD,	57
THE HOUR OF PRAYER,	HEMANS,	60
PRAYER,	BP. MANT,	62
A GLEAM OF SUNSHINE,	LONGFELLOW,	63
THE SABBATH BELL,	ANON.,	66
SUNDAY,	HART. COLERIDGE,	68
SUNDAY,	CLARE,	69
THE VOICE OF PRAYER,	ANON.,	73
THE LORD'S DAY,	BP. MANT,	75
THERE IS A TONGUE IN EVERY LEAF,	ANON.,	76
A SUNDAY THOUGHT,	ANON.,	77
A DOMESTIC SCENE,	HEMANS,	78
THE SABBATH BELLS,	CHARLES LAMB,	79
THE SABBATH ON THE SEAS,	GODWIN,	80
THE SABBATH EVE,	ANON.,	82
THE SAILOR'S EVENING PRAYER,	ANON.,	84
THE FIRST SABBATH,	GRAHAME,	85
A WINTER SABBATH WALK,	GRAHAME,	88
THE NIGHT WAS WINTER,	COWPER,	90
EARLY RISING AND PRAYER,	VAUGHAN,	92
THE SABBATH,	GRAHAME,	94

CONTENTS.

		PAGE
THE COVENANTERS' SABBATH	WEIR,	97
A SABBATH MEDITATION,	LEYDEN,	101
SABBATH EVENING,	EDMESTON,	102
SABBATH WALKS,	CLARE,	104
HOW SWEET THE TUNEFUL BELL,	BOWLES,	105
OF ALL THE MURDEROUS TRADES,	GRAHAME,	106
SUNDAYS,	VAUGHAN,	107
THE SABBATH,	EAST,	108
AN EVENING HYMN,	THOMAS MILLER,	109
THE TIME FOR PRAYER,	ANON.,	113
SOCIAL WORSHIP,	BP. MANT,	114
THE CURFEW BELL,	LONGFELLOW,	115
THE SABBATH,	DA COSTA,	117
EVENING PRAYER,	HEMANS,	118
THE NIGHT-WATCHMAN'S SONG,	ANON.,	120
CHURCH MUSIC,	HERBERT,	124
A PLACE FOR SOCIAL PRAYER,	COWPER,	125
PRAISE.	HERBERT,	127

SABBATH BELLS.

THE SABBATH.

How still the morning of the hallowed day!
Mute is the voice of rural labor, hushed
The plough-boy's whistle, and the milk-maid's song.
The scythe lies glittering in the dewy wreath
Of tedded grass, mingled with fading flowers,
That yester-morn bloomed waving in the breeze.
Sounds the most faint attract the ear,—the hum
Of early bee, the trickling of the dew,
The distant bleating midway up the hill.
Calmness sits throned on yon unmoving cloud.
To him who wanders o'er the upland leas,
The blackbird's note comes mellower from the dale;
And sweeter from the sky the gladsome lark
Warbles his heaven-tuned song; the lulling brook
Murmurs more gently down the deep-worn glen;

While from yon lowly roof, whose curling smoke
O'ermounts the mist, is heard, at intervals,
The voice of psalms—the simple song of praise.

With dove-like wings, Peace o'er yon village broods:
The dizzying mill-wheel rests; the anvil's din
Hath ceased; all, all around is quietness.
Less fearful on this day, the limping hare
Stops, and looks back, and stops, and looks on man,
Her deadliest foe. The toil-worn horse, set free,
Unheedful of the pasture, roams at large;
And, as his stiff unwieldy bulk he rolls,
His iron-armed hoofs gleam in the morning ray.

But chiefly man the day of rest enjoys.
Hail, SABBATH! thee I hail, the poor man's day.
On other days the man of toil is doomed
To eat his joyless bread, lonely; the ground
Both seat and board; screened from the winter's cold,
And summer's heat, by neighboring hedge or tree;
But on this day, embosomed in his home,
He shares the frugal meal with those he loves;
With those he loves he shares the heartfelt joy

A word and a grimace, but reverently,
With covered face and upward earnest eye.

   Hail, SABBATH! thee I hail, the poor man's day:
The pale mechanic now has leave to breathe
The morning air, pure from the city's smoke;
While, wandering slowly up the river side,
He meditates on HIM, whose power he marks
In each green tree that proudly spreads the bough,
As in the tiny dew-bent flowers that bloom
Around its roots; and while he thus surveys,
With elevated joy, each rural charm,
He hopes, yet fears presumption in the hope,
That Heaven may be one SABBATH without end.

   But now his steps a welcome sound recalls:
Solemn the knell, from yonder ancient pile,
Fills all the air, inspiring joyful awe:
Slowly the throng moves o'er the tomb-paved ground:
The aged man, the bowed down, the blind
Led by the thoughtless boy, and he who breathes
With pain, and eyes the new-made grave well
    pleased;

These, mingled with the young, the gay, approach
The house of God; these, spite of all their ills,
A glow of gladness feel; with silent praise
They enter in.
GRAHAME

SUNDAY.

Oh day most calm, most bright,
The fruit of this, the next world's bud,
The indorsement of supreme delight,
Writ by a Friend, and with His blood;
The couch of time; care's balm and bay;
The week were dark, but for thy light:
    Thy torch doth show the way.

The other days and thou
Make up one man; whose face thou art,
Knocking at heaven with thy brow:
The working days are the back part;
The burden of the week lies there,
Making the whole to stoop and bow,
    Till thy release appear.

Man had straight forward gone
To endless death; but thou dost pull
And turn us round to look on One,
Whom, if we were not very dull,
We could not choose but look on still;
Since there is no place so alone,
    The which He doth not fill.

Sundays the pillars are,
On which Heaven's palace arched lies:
The other days fill up the spare
And hollow room with vanities.
They are the fruitful beds and borders
In God's rich garden: that is bare
    Which parts their ranks and orders

The Sundays of man's life,
Thredded together on time's string,
Make bracelets to adorn the wife
Of the eternal glorious King.
On Sunday Heaven's gate stands ope;
Blessings are plentiful and rife,
    More plentiful than hope!

SUNDAY.

This day my Saviour rose,
And did enclose this light for his:
That, as each beast his manger knows,
Man might not of his fodder miss.
Christ hath took in this piece of ground,
And made a garden there for those
  Who want herbs for their wound.

The rest of our creation
Our great Redeemer did remove
With the same shake, which at his passion,
Did the earth and all things with it move.
As Samson bore the doors away,
Christ's hands, though nailed, wrought our sa'vation,
  And did unhinge that day.

The brightness of that day
We sullied by our foul offence:
Wherefore that robe we cast away,
Having a new at his expense:
Whose drops of blood paid the full price,
That was required to make us gay,
  And fit for paradise.

Thou art a day of mirth :
And where the week-days trail on ground,
Thy flight is higher, as thy birth :
O let me take thee at the bound,
Leaping with thee from seven to seven,
Till that we both, being tossed from earth,
Fly hand in hand to Heaven !
George Herbert.

SABBATH MORNING.

How beautiful the Sunday morn, amid
The quietude of nature ! Spreading trees
And the simplicity of rural life
Best harmonize with its divine intent ;
And more than pompous cities, or the throngs
That flow unceasing through their crowded streets,
Welcome its silent spirit. Here, and there,
A rustic houschold, toward the village church
Wind through green lanes, where still the dewy
    grass
Reserves its diamonds for them. Happy sire,
And peaceful grandsire, with his hoary hair,

And joyous children, their fresh ruddy brows
Composed to serious thought, and even the babe
In its young innocence, a wondering guest,
Wend forth, in blessed company, to pay
Their vows to Him, who heeds "the pure in heart."
SIGOURNEY.

A SPRING SABBATH WALK.

Oh how I love, with melted soul, to leave
The house of prayer, and wander in the fields
Alone! What though the opening spring be chill!
Although the lark, checked in his airy path,
Eke out his song, perched on the fallow clod,
That still o'ertops the blade! Although no branch
Have spread its foliage, save the willow wand,
That dips its pale leaves in the swollen stream!
What though the clouds oft lower! Their threats but end
In sunny showers, that scarcely fill the folds
Of moss-couched violet, or interrupt
The merle's dulcet pipe,—melodious bird!
He, hid behind the milk-white sloe-thorn spray,

(Whose early flowers anticipate the leaf,)
Welcomes the time of buds, the infant year.

Sweet is the sunny nook, to which my steps
Have brought me, hardly conscious where I roamed,
Unheeding where,—so lovely all around,
The works of GOD, arrayed in vernal smile.

Oft at this season, musing, I prolong
My devious range, till, sunk from view, the sun
Emblaze, with upward-slanting ray, the breast
And wing unquivering of the wheeling lark,
Descending, vocal, from her latest flight;
While, disregardful of yon lonely star,—
The harbinger of chill night's glittering host,—
Sweet Red-breast, SCOTIA's Philomela, chants,
In desultory strains, his evening hymn.
GRAHAME.

THE HOUSE OF GOD.

IT is the Sabbath bell, which calls to prayer,
  Even to the House of God, the hallowed dome,
  Where He who claims it bids His people come
To bow before His throne, and serve Him there

With prayers, and thanks, and praises. Some there
    are
  Who hold it meet to linger now at home,
  And some o'er fields and the wide hills to roam,
And worship in the temple of the air!
For me, not heedless of the lone address,
  Nor slack to greet my Maker on the height,
By wood, or living stream; yet not the less
  Seek I His presence in each social rite
Of His own temple: *that* He deigns to bless,
  There still he dwells, and *there* is His delight.

BP. MANT

ENGLISH CHURCHES.

How beautiful they stand,
Those ancient altars of our native land!
Amid the pasture fields and dark green woods,
Amid the mountain's cloudy solitudes;
By rivers broad that rush into the sea;
  By little brooks that, with a lapsing sound,
Like playful children, run by copse and lea!
  Each in its little plot of holy ground,
How beautiful they stand,
Those old gray churches o' our native land!

Our lives are all turmoil;
Our souls are in a weary strife and toil,
Grasping and straining—tasking nerve and brain,
Both day and night, for gain!
We have grown worldly—have made gold our god—
    Have turned our hearts away from lowly things;
We seek not now the wild flower on the sod;
    We seek not snowy-folded angel's wings
Amid the summer skies—
For visions come not to polluted eyes!

    Yet, blessed quiet fanes!
Still piety, still poetry remains,
And shall remain, whilst ever on the air
One chapel-bell calls high and low to prayer,—
Whilst ever green and sunny churchyards keep
    The dust of our beloved, and tears are shed
From founts which in the human heart lie deep!
    Something in these aspiring days we need,
To keep our spirits lowly,
To set within our hearts sweet thoughts and holy!

    And 'tis for this they stand,
The old gray churches of our native land!

And even in the gold-corrupted mart,
In the great city's heart,
They stand; and chantry dim, and organ sound,
    And stated services of prayer and praise,
Like to the righteous ten which were not found
    For the polluted city, shall upraise,
Meek faith and love sincere—
Better in time of need than shield and spear!

L. E. Landon.

*   *   *   *

'Tis sweet to hear a brook, 'tis sweet
    To hear the Sabbath-bell,
'Tis sweet to hear them both at once,
    Deep in a woody dell.

Coleridge.

A CHURCHYARD SCENE.

How sweet and solemn, all alone,
With revered step, from stone to stone,
In a small village churchyard lying,
O'er intervening flowers to move—

And as we read the names unknown,
Of young and old, to judgment gone,
And hear, in the calm air above,
Time onward, softly flying,
To meditate, in Christian love,
Upon the dead and dying!
Across the silence, seem to go
With dream-like motion, wavery, slow,
And shrouded in their folds of snow,
The friends we loved long, long ago!
Gliding across the sad retreat,
How beautiful their phantom feet!
What tenderness is in their eyes,
Turned where the poor survivor lies,
'Mid monitory sanctities!
What years of vanished joy are fanned
From one uplifting of that hand
In its white stillness! When the shade
Doth glimmeringly in sunshine fade
From our embrace, how dim appears
This world's life, through a mist of tears!
Vain hopes! Wild sorrows! Needless fears!
Such is the scene around me now:
A little churchyard, on the brow

A CHURCHYARD SCENE.

Of a green pastoral hill:
Its sylvan village sleeps below,
And faintly, here, is heard the flow
Of Woodburn's summer rill;
A place where all things mournful meet,
And yet, the sweetest of the sweet!—
The stillest of the still!
With what a pensive beauty fall,
Across the mossy, mouldering wall
That rose-tree's clustered arches! See
The robin-redbreast, warily,
Bright through the blossoms leaves his nest:
Sweet ingrate! through the winter blest
At the firesides of men—but shy
Through all the sunny, summer hours—
He hides himself among the flowers
In his own wild festivity.
What lulling sound, and shadow cool,
Hangs half the darkened churchyard o'er,
From thy green depth, so beautiful,
Thou gorgeous sycamore!
Oft hath the lonely wine and bread
Been blessed beneath thy murmuring tent,
Where many a bright and hoary head

Bowed at the awful sacrament.
Now all beneath the turf are laid,
On which they sat, and sang, and prayed.
Above that consecrated tree
Ascends the tapering spire, that seems
To lift the soul up silently
To heaven with all its dreams!—
While in the belfry, deep and low,
From his heaved bosom's purple gleams
The dove's continuous murmurs flow,
A dirge-like song, half bliss, half woe,—
The voice so lonely seems!

JOHN WILSON.

A SUMMER SABBATH WALK.

DELIGHTFUL is this loneliness; it calms
My heart: pleasant the cool beneath these elms,
That throw across the stream a moveless shade.
Here nature in her midnoon whisper speaks:
How peaceful every sound!—the ring-dove's plaint,
Moaned from the twilight centre of the grove,
While every other woodland lay is mute,
Save when the wren flits from her down-coved nest,

And from the root-sprig trills her ditty clear,—
The grasshopper's oft-pausing chirp,—the buzz,
Angrily shrill, of moss-entangled bee,
That, soon as loosed, booms with full twang away,—
The sudden rushing of the minnow shoal,
Scared from the shallows by my passing tread.

      Grateful the breeze
That fans my throbbing temples! smiles the plain
Spread wide below: how sweet the placid view!
But oh! more sweet the thought, heart-soothing
  thought,
That thousands, and ten thousands of the sons
Of toil, partake this day the common joy
Of rest, of peace, of viewing hill and dale,
Of breathing in the silence of the woods,
And blessing Him, who gave the Sabbath day.
Yes, my heart flutters with a freer throb,
To think that now the townsman wanders forth
Among the fields and meadows, to enjoy
The coolness of the day's decline; to see
His children sport around, and simply pull
The flower and weed promiscuous, as a boon,
Which proudly in his breast they smiling fix.

         GRAHAME.

THE VILLAGE CHURCH.

Morning and Evening brings
Its holy office; and the Sabbath-bell,
That over wood and wild and mountain dell
Wanders so far, chasing all thoughts unholy
With sounds most musical, most melancholy,
Not on his ear is lost.—Then he pursues
The pathway leading through the aged yews,
Nor unattended, and when all are there,
Pours out his spirit in the House of Prayer.
Rogers.

THE SABBATH.

What spell has o'er the populous city past!
  The wonted current of its life is stayed:
Its sports, its gainful schemes, are earthward cast,
  As though their vileness were at once displayed:
The roar of trade has ceased, and on the air
Come holy songs and solemn sounds of prayer.

Far spreads the charm! from every hamlet spire
  A note of rest and heavenward thought is pealed:

By his calm hearth reclines the peasant sire;
  The toil-worn steed basks in the breezy field.
Within, without, through farm and cottage blest,
'Tis one bright day of gladness and of rest.

Down from the mountain dwellings, while the dew
  Shines on the heath-bells, and the fern is bending
In the fresh breeze, in festive garbs I view
  Childhood and age and buoyant youth descending.
God! who hast piled thy wonders round their home,
'Tis in their love they to thy temple come.

A stately ship speeds o'er the mighty main—
  Oh, many a league from our own happy land:
Yet from its heart ascends the choral strain;
  For there its little isolated band,
Amid the ocean desert's awful roar,
Praise Him whose love links shore to distant shore.

O'er palmy woods where summer radiance falls,
  In the glad islands of the Indian main,
What thronging crowds the missionary calls
  To raise to heaven the Christian's glorious strain!
Lo! where, engirt by children of the sun,
Stands the white man, and counts his victories won.

In the fierce deserts of a distant zone,
  'Mid savage nations terrible and stern,
A lonely atom, severed from his own,
  The traveller wends, death or renown to earn.
Parched, fasting, wearied, verging to despair,
He kneels, he prays—hope kindles in his prayer.

O'er the wide world, blest day, thine influence flies;
  Rest o'er the sufferer spreads her balmy wings;
Love wakes, joy dawns, praise fills the listening skies;
  Th' expanding heart from earth's enchantment springs:—
Heaven for one day withdraws its ancient ban,
Unbars its gates and dwells once more with man.

WILLIAM HOWITT.

SUNDAY WALKS.

How fond the rustic's ear at leisure dwells
On the soft soundings of his village bells,
  As on a Sunday morning at his ease
  He takes his rambles, just as fancies please,

Down narrow balks that intersect the fields,
Hid in profusion that its produce yields:
Long twining peas, in faintly misted greens;
And winged-leaf multitudes of crowding beans;
And flighty oatlands of a lighter hue;
And speary barley bowing down with dew;
And browning wheat-ear, on its taper stalk,
With gentle breezes bending o'er the balk,
Greeting the parting hand that brushes near
With patting welcomes of a plenteous year.
Or narrow lanes, where cool and gloomy sweet
Hedges above head in an arbor meet,
Meandering down, and resting for a while
Upon a moss-clad molehill or a stile;
While every scene that on his leisure crowds,
Wind-waving valleys and light passing clouds,
In brighter colors seems to meet the eye,
Than in the bustle of the days gone by.
A peaceful solitude around him creeps,
And nature seemly o'er her quiet sleeps;
No noise is heard, save sutherings through the trees
Of brisk wind gushes, or a trembling breeze;
And song of linnets in the hedge-row thorn,
Twittering their welcomes to the day's return;

And hum of bees, where labor's doomed to stray
In ceaseless bustle on his weary way;
And low of distant cattle here and there,
Seeking the stream, or dropping down to lair;
And bleat of sheep, and horses' playful neigh,
From rustic's whips, and plough, and wagon, free,
Baiting in careless freedom o'er the leas,
Or turned to knap each other at their ease.
While 'neath the bank on which he rests his head
The brook mourns drippling o'er its pebbly bed,
And whimpers soothingly a calm serene
O'er the lulled comforts of a Sunday scene,
He ponders round, and muses with a smile
On thriving produce of his earlier toil;
What once were kernels from his hopper sown,
Now browning wheat-ears and oat-bunches grown,
And pea-pods swelled, by blossoms long forsook,
And nearly ready for the scythe and hook:
He pores with wonder on the mighty change
Which suns and showers perform, and thinks it
    strange;
And though no philosophic reasoning draws,
His music marvels home to nature's cause,
A simple feeling in him turns his eye

To where the thin clouds smoke along the sky;
And there his soul consents the Power must reign
Who rules the year, and shoots the spindling grain,
Lights up the sun, and sprinkles rain below—
The Fount of nature whence all causes flow.
Thus much the feeling of his bosom warms,
Nor seeks he farther than his soul informs.

A six-days' prisoner, life's support to earn
From dusty cobwebs and the murky barn,
The weary thresher meets the rest that's given,
And thankful soothes him in the boon of heaven;
But happier still in Sabbath walks he feels,
With love's sweet pledges poddling at his heels,
That oft divert him with their childish glee
In fruitless chases after bird and bee;
And, eager gathering every flower they pass
Of yellow lambtoe and the totter-grass,
Oft whimper round him disappointment's sigh
At sight of blossom that's in bloom too high,
And twitch his sleeve with all their coaxing powers
To urge his hand to reach the tempting flowers:
Then as he climbs, their eager hopes to crown,
On gate or stile to pull the blossoms down

Of pale hedge-roses straggling wild and tall,
And scrambling woodbines that outgrow them all,
He turns to days when he himself would tease
His tender father for such toys as these,
And smiles with rapture, as he plucks the flowers,
To meet the feelings of those lovely hours,
And blesses Sunday's rest, whose peace at will
Retains a portion of those pleasures still.

But when the duty of the day's expired,
And priest and parish offer what's required,
When godly farmer shuts his book again
To talk of profits from advancing grain,
Short memory keeping what the parson read,
Prayers 'neath his arm, and business in his head;
And, dread of boys, the clerk is left to close
The creaking church-door on its week's repose;
Then leave me Sunday's remnant to employ
In seeking sweets of solitary joy,
And lessons learning from a simple tongue,
Where nature preaches in a cricket's song;
Where every tiny thing that flies and creeps,
  Some feeble language owns, its prayer to raise;
Where all that lives, by noise or silence, keeps
  A homely Sabbath in its Maker's praise.

SUNDAY WALKS.

There, free from labor, let my musings stray
Where footpaths ramble from the public way
In quiet loneliness o'er many a scene,
Through grassy close, or grounds of blossomed bean;
Oft winding balks where groves of willows spread
Their welcome waving shadows over-head,
And thorns beneath in woodbines often drest
Inviting strongly in their peace to rest;
Or wildly left to follow choice at will
O'er many a trackless vale and pathless hill,
Or, nature's wilderness, o'er heaths of goss,
Each footstep sinking ankle-deep in moss,
By pleasing interruptions often tied,
A hedge to clamber or a brook to stride;
Where no approaching feet or noises rude
Molest the quiet of one's solitude,
Save birds, their song broke by a false alarm,
Through branches fluttering from their fancied
    harm;
And cows and sheep with startled low and bleat
Disturbed from lair by one's unwelcome feet,—
The all that's met in Sunday's slumbering ease,
That adds to, more than checks the power to please.

THE NEW YORK
PUBLIC LIBRARY.

ASTOR, LENOX AND
TILDEN FOUNDATIONS.

SUNDAY WALKS.

And sweet it is to creep one's blinded way
Where woodland boughs shut out the smiles of day,
Where, hemmed in glooms that scarce give leave to spy
A passing cloud or patch of purple sky,
We track, half hidden from the world besides,
Sweet hermit-nature that in woodlands hides;
Where nameless flowers that never meet the sun,
Like bashful modesty, the sight to shun,
Bud in their snug retreat, and bloom, and die,
Without one notice of a passing eye;
There, while I drop me in the woody waste
'Neath arbors Nature fashions to her taste,
Entwining oak-trees with the ivy's gloom,
And woodbines propping over boughs to bloom,
And scalloped briony mingling round her bowers,
Whose fine bright leaves make up the want of flowers,—
With nature's minstrels of the woods let me,
Thou Lord of Sabbaths, add a song to thee,
An humble offering for the holy day
  Which thou most wise and graciously hast given,
As leisure dropt in labor's rugged way
  To claim a passport with the rest to heaven.

CLARE.

THE SABBATH.

Fresh glides the brook and blows the gale,
    Yet yonder halts the quiet mill;
The whirring wheel, the rushing sail,
    How motionless and still!

Six days of toil, poor child of Cain,
    Thy strength the slave of Want may be;
The seventh thy limbs escape the chain—
    A God hath made thee free!

Ah, tender was the law that gave
    This holy respite to the breast,
To breathe the gale, to watch the wave,
    And know—the wheel may rest!

But where the waves the gentlest glide,
    What image charms to lift thine eyes?
The spire reflected on the tide
    Invites thee to the skies.

To teach the soul its nobler worth,
    This rest from mortal toils is given;
Go, snatch the brief reprieve from earth,
    And pass—a guest to heaven.

They tell thee, in their dreaming school,
   Of power from old dominion hurled,
When rich and poor, with juster rule,
   Shall share the altered world.

Alas! since Time itself began,
   That fable hath but fooled the hour;
Each age that ripens power in man,
   But subjects man to power.

Yet every day in seven, at least,
   One bright republic shall be known;—
Man's world awhile hath surely ceased,
   When God proclaims his own!

Six days may Rank divide the poor,
   O Dives, from thy banquet hall—
The seventh the Father opes the door,
   And holds His feast for all!

Sir E. Bulwer Lytton

THE SABBATH.

Dear is the hallowed morn to me,
   When village bells awake the day;

THE SABBATH.

And by their sacred minstrelsy,
   Call me from earthly cares away.

And dear to me the winged hour,
   Spent in thy hallowed courts, O Lord—
To feel devotion's soothing power,
   And catch the manna of thy Word.

And dear to me the loud Amen
   Which echoes through the blest abode,
Which swells, and sinks, and swells again,
   Dies on the walls, but lives to God.

And dear the simple melody,
   Sung with the pomp of rustic art,
That holy, heavenly harmony,
   The music of a thankful heart.

In secret I have often prayed,
   And still the anxious tear would fall;
But, on the sacred altar laid,
   The fire descends and dries them all.

Oft when the world, with iron hands,
   Has bound me in its six days' chain,

This burst them, like the strong man's bands,
   And let my spirit loose again.

Then, dear to me, the Sabbath morn,
   The village bells, the shepherd's voice,
These oft have found my heart forlorn,
   And always bid that heart rejoice.

Go, man of pleasure, strike the lyre,
   Of Sabbaths broken sing the charms;
Ours are the prophet's car of fire,
   Which bears us to a Father's arms.

CUNNINGHAM.

THE CHURCHYARD.

The thought of early death was in my heart,
   Of the cold grave, and "dumb forgetfulness;"
     And with a weight like lead,
     An overwhelming dread
Mysteriously my spirit did oppress.

And forth I roamed in that distressful mood,
   Abroad into the sultry, sunless day;

      All hung with one huge cloud,
      That like a sable shroud
On Nature's deep sepulchral stillness lay.

Black fell the shadows of the churchyard elms,
   (Instinctively my feet had wandered there,)
      And through that awful gloom,
      Headstone and altar tomb,
Among the dark heaps gleamed with ghastlier glare.

Death, death was in my heart, as there I stood;
   Mine eyes fast fixed on a grass-grown mound;
      As though they would descry
      The loathsome mystery
Consummating beneath that charnel ground.

Death, death was in my heart—Methought I felt
   A heavy hand that pressed me down below—
      And some resistless power
      Made me in that dark hour,
Half long to *be*, where I abhorred to *go*.

Then suddenly—albeit no breeze was felt—
   Through the tall tree-tops ran a shivering sound—

Forth from the western heaven
Flashed out a flaming levin,
And one long thunder-peal rolled echoing round.

One long, long-echoing peal, and all was peace—
  Cool rain-drops gemmed the herbage—large and few;
    And that dull vault of lead
    Disparting overhead,
  Down beamed an eye of soft celestial blue.

And up towards the heavenly portal sprang
  A skylark, scattering off the feathery rain;
    Up, from my very feet—
    And oh! how clear and sweet
Rang through the fields of air his mountain strain!

"Blithe, blessed creature! take me there with thee!"
  I cried in spirit—passionately cried—
    But higher still, and higher
    Rang out that living lyre,
  As if the bird disdained me in its pride.

And I was left below, but now no more
   Plunged in the doleful realms of death and night;
      Up with the skylark's lay
      My soul had winged its way
To the supernal Source of life and light.
Miss Bowles.

THE VILLAGE CHURCH.

Dear is the ancient village church, which rears
   By the lone yew, on lime or elm-girt mound,
   Its modest fabric: dear, 'mid pleasant sound
Of bells, the gray embattled tower, that wears,
Of changeful hue, the marks of bygone years;
   Buttress, and porch, and arch with mazy round
   Of curious fret or shapes fantastic crowned;
Tall pinnacles, and mingled window-tiers,
Norman, or misnamed Gothic. Fairer spot
Thou givest not, England, to the tasteful eye,
Nor to the heart more soothing. Blest their lot,
   Knew they their bliss, who own, their dwelling nigh,
Such resting-place; there, by the world forgot,
   In life to worship, and, when dead, to lie!
Bp Mant.

* * * * *

THEY pursue the pebbly walk
    That leads to the white porch the Sunday throng,
Hand-coupled urchins in restrained talk,
    And anxious pedagogue that chastens wrong,
And posied churchwarden with solemn stalk,
    And gold-bedizened beadle flames along,
And gentle peasant clad in buff and green,
Like a meek cowslip in the spring serene;

And blushing maiden,—modestly arrayed
    In spotless white,—still conscious of the glass;
And she, the lonely widow, that hath made
    A sable covenant with grief,—alas!
She veils her tears under the deep, deep shade,
    While the poor kindly-hearted, as they pass,
Bend to unclouded childhood, and caress
Her boy!—so rosy!—and so fatherless!

Thus, as good Christians ought, they all draw near
    The fair white temple, to the timely call

Of pleasant bells that tremble in the ear.—
    Now the last frock, and scarlet hood, and shawl
Fade into dusk, in the dim atmosphere
Of the low porch, and heaven has won them all.
Hood

THE CHURCH BELLS.

What varying sounds from yon gray pinnacles
    Sweep o'er the ear, and claim the heart's reply!
    Now the blithe peal of home festivity,
Natal or nuptial, in full concert swells:
Now the brisk chime, or voice of altered bells,
    Speaks the due hour of social worship nigh:
    And now the last stage of mortality
The deep dull toll with lingering warning tells.
How much of human life those sounds comprise;
    Birth, wedded love, God's service, and the tomb!
Heard not in vain, if thence kind feelings rise,
    Such as befit our being, free from gloom
Monastic,—prayer that communes with the skies,
    And musings mindful of the final doom.
Bp. Mant

AN AUTUMN·SABBATH WALK.

WHEN homeward bands their several ways disperse,
I love to linger in the narrow field
Of rest; to wander round from tomb to tomb,
And think of some who silent sleep below.
Sad sighs the wind, that from those ancient elms
Shakes showers of leaves upon the withered grass:
The sere and yellow wreaths, with eddying sweep,
Fill up the furrows 'tween the hillocked graves.
But list that moan! 'tis the poor blind man's dog,
His guide for many a day, now come to mourn
The master and the friend—conjunction rare!
A man he was indeed of gentle soul,
Though bred to brave the deep: the lightning's flash
Had dimmed, not closed, his mild, but sightless eyes
He was a welcome guest through all his range;
(It was not wide:) no dog would bay at him:
Children would run to meet him on his way,
And lead him to a sunny seat, and climb
His knee, and wonder at his oft-told tales.
Then would he teach the elfins how to plait

The rushy cap and crown, or sedgy ship;
And I have seen him lay his tremulous hand
Upon their heads, while silent moved his lips.
Peace to thy spirit! that now looks on me,
Perhaps with greater pity than I felt
To see thee wandering darkling on thy way.
GRAHAME.

SABBATH DAYS.

MODERNIZED FROM "SON-DAYES," IN VAUGHAN'S
"SILEX SCINTILLANS."

TYPES of eternal rest—fair buds of bliss,
  In heavenly flowers unfolding week by week—
The next world's gladness imaged forth in this—
  Days of whose worth the Christian's heart can speak!

Eternity in time—the steps by which
  We climb to future ages—lamps that light
Man through his darker days, and thought enrich,
  Yielding redemption for the week's dull flight.

Wakeners of prayer in man—his resting bowers
   As on he journeys in the narrow way,
Where, Eden-like, Jehovah's walking hours
   Are waited for as in the cool of day.

Days fixed by God for intercourse with dust,
   To raise our thoughts and purify our powers—
Periods appointed to renew our trust—
   A gleam of glory after six days' showers!

A milky way marked out through skies else drear,
   By radiant suns that warm as well as shine—
A clue, which he who follows knows no fear,
   Though briers and thorns around his pathway twine.

Foretastes of heaven on earth—pledges of joy
   Surpassing fancy's flights, and fiction's story—
The preludes of a feast that cannot cloy,
   And the bright out-courts of immortal glory!

                          BARTON.

* * * *

How soft the music of those village bells,
Falling at intervals upon the ear
In cadence sweet, now dying all away,
Now pealing loud again, and louder still,
Clear and sonorous, as the gale comes on!
With easy force it opens all the cells
Where Memory slept. Wherever I have heard
A kindred melody, the scene recurs,
And with it all its pleasures and its pains.
Such comprehensive views the spirit takes,
That in a few short moments I retrace
(As in a map the voyager his course)
The windings of my way through many years.

Cowper.

THE BELL.

I love the bell that calls the poor to pray,
   Chiming from village church its cheerful sound,
When the sun smiles on Labor's holy-day,
   And all the rustic train are gathered round,
Each deftly dizened in his Sunday's best,
And pleased to hail the day of piety and rest.

THE NEW YORK
PUBLIC LIBRARY.

ASTOR, LENOX AND
TILDEN FOUNDATIONS.

And when, dim shadowing o'er the face of day,
   The mantling mists of eventide rise slow,
As through the forest gloom I wend my way,
   The minster curfew's sullen voice I know,
And pause, and love its solemn toll to hear,
As made by distance soft it dies upon the ear.

Nor with an idle nor unwilling ear
   Do I receive the early passing bell;
For, sick at heart with many a secret care,
   When I lie listening to the dead man's knell,
I think that in the grave all sorrows cease,
And would full fain recline my head and be at peace.
    *   *   *   *   *

                      SOUTHEY.

THE VILLAGE CHURCH.

MINE be the rude and artless pile,
   The ivy-mantled turret gray,
Within whose old unsculptured aisle,
   The toil-worn peasant kneels to pray;
The whitened wall, the latticed pane,
   The rustic porch, the oaken door;

Above, the rafters huge and plain,
    Beneath, the footstep-graven floor.

Not here, where few could pomp admire,
    The sons of wealth their pomp display;
They throng not here in gay attire,
    Who come to gaze and not to pray:
No high-tuned choral peals surprise,
    Enchanting fashion's languid train,
With arts ingenious to disguise
    The bard of Sion's raptured strain.

But here, where lowly hearts are bowed,
    By toil and sorrows gentler made,
Nor earth-born schemes, nor visions proud,
    The unambitious breast invade;
More nearly is His presence felt,
    For whom the Heaven of Heaven expands
Its arch in vain, who never dwelt
    In temples built by human hands.

By viewless Spirit of the air
    The soul's mysterious depths are stirred,
More fervent soars the heavenward prayer,
    More deeply sinks the engrafted word:

Oh! could my heart, in darker hour,
That calm and reverent mood recall,
How weak were then temptation's power,
How frail the world's unhallowed thrall!

ANON.

THE DAY OF REST.

Return, thou wished and welcome guest,
Thou day of holiness and rest;
The best, the dearest of the seven,
Emblem and harbinger of heaven;
Though not the Bridegroom, at His voice,
Friend of the Bridegroom, still rejoice.
Day, doubly sanctified and blessed,
Thee the Creator crowned with rest;
From all His works, from all His woes,
On thee the Saviour found repose.
Thou dost, with mystic voice, rehearse
The birth-day of a universe;
Prophet, historian, both, in scope
Thou speak'st to memory and to hope.
    Amidst the earthliness of life,
Vexation, vanity and strife,

THE DAY OF REST.

Sabbath! how sweet thy holy calm
Comes o'er the soul, like healing balm;
Comes like the dew to fainting flowers,
Renewing her enfeebled powers.
Thine hours, how soothingly they glide,
Thy morn, thy noon, thine eventide!
All meet as brethren, mix as friends.
Nature her general groan suspends;
No cares the sin-born laborers tire;
E'en the poor brutes thou bid'st respire:
'Tis almost as, restored awhile,
Earth had resumed her Eden smile.
I love thy call of earthly bells,
As on my waking ear it swells;
I love to see thy pious train
Seeking in groups the solemn fane:
But most I love to mingle there
In sympathy of praise and prayer,
And listening to that living Word,
Which breathes the spirit of the Lord:
Or at the mystic table placed,
Those eloquent mementoes taste
Of Thee, Thou suffering Lamb Divine,
Thou soul-refreshing bread and wine;

Sweet viands given us to assuage
The faintness of the pilgrimage.
  Severed from Salem, while unstrung
His harp on Pagan willows hung,
What wonder if the Psalmist pined,
As for her brooks the hunted hind!—
The temple's humblest place should win
Gladlier than all the pomp of sin;—
Envied th' unconscious birds that sung
Around those altars, o'er their young;
And deemed one heavenly Sabbath worth
More than a thousand days of earth;
Well might his heart and harp rejoice
To hear, once more, that festal voice;
"Come, brethren, come with glad accord,
Haste to the dwelling of the Lord."
  But if on earth so calm, so blest,
The house of prayer, the day of rest;
If to the spirit when it faints,
So sweet the assembly of the saints;—
There let us pitch our tents (we say),
For, Lord, with Thee 'tis good to stay!
Yet from the mount we soon descend,
Too soon our earthly Sabbaths end;

Cares of a work-day will return,
And faint our hearts, and fitful, burn;
Oh! think, my soul! beyond compare,
Think what a Sabbath must be there,
Where all is holy bliss, that knows
Nor imperfection, nor a close;
Where that innumerable throng
Of saints and angels mingle song;
Where, wrought with hands, no temples rise,
For God Himself their place supplies;
Nor priests are needed in the abode
Where the whole hosts are priests to God.
Think what a Sabbath *there* shall be,—
The Sabbath of Eternity!

GRINFIELD.

THE HOUR OF PRAYER.

CHILD, amidst the flowers at play,
While the red light fades away;
Mother, with thine earnest eye
Ever following silently;
Father, by the breeze of eve
Called thy harvest work to leave—

THE HOUR OF PRAYER.

Pray: ere yet the dark hours be,
Lift the heart and bend the knee!

Traveller, in the stranger's land,
Far from thine own household band;
Mourner, haunted by the tone
Of a voice from this world gone;
Captive, in whose narrow cell
Sunshine hath not leave to dwell;
Sailor, on the darkening sea—
Lift the heart and bend the knee!

Warrior, that from battle won
Breathest now at set of sun;
Woman, o'er the lowly slain
Weeping on his burial-plain;
Ye that triumph, ye that sigh,
Kindred by one holy tie,
Heaven's first star alike ye see—
Lift the heart and bend the knee!

HEMANS

PRAYER.

Ere the morning's busy ray
Call you to your work away;
Ere the silent evening close
Your wearied eyes in sweet repose,
To lift your heart and voice in prayer
Be your *first* and *latest* care.

He, to whom the prayer is due,
From heaven His throne shall smile on you;
Angels sent by Him shall tend,
Your daily labor to befriend,
And their nightly vigils keep
To guard you in the hour of sleep.

When through the peaceful parish swells
The music of the Sabbath bells,
Duly tread the sacred road
Which leads you to the house of God;
The blessing of the Lamb is there,
And "God is in the midst of her."

PRAYER.

And oh! where'er your days be past,
And oh! howe'er your lot be cast,
Still think on Him whose eye surveys,
Whose hand is over all your ways.
Abroad, at home, in weal, in woe,
That service which to Heaven you owe,
That bounden service duly pay,
And God shall be your strength alway.

He only to the heart can give
Peace and true pleasure while you live;
He only, when you yield your breath,
Can guide you through the vale of death.

He can, He will, from out the dust
Raise the blest spirits of the just;
Heal every wound, hush every fear,
From every eye wipe every tear;
And place them where distress is o'er,
And pleasures dwell for evermore.

Bp. Mant.

A GLEAM OF SUNSHINE.

THIS is the place. Stand still, my steed,
    Let me review the scene,
And summon from the shadowy Past
    The forms that once have been.

The Past and Present here unite,
    Beneath time's flowing tide,
Like footprints hidden by a brook,
    But seen on either side.

Here runs the highway to the town;
    There the green lane descends,
Through which I walked to church with thee,
    O gentlest of my friends!

The shadow of the linden-trees
    Lay moving on the grass;
Between them and the moving boughs,
    A shadow, thou didst pass.

Thy dress was like the lilies,
    And thy heart as pure as they;
One of God's holy messengers
    Did walk with me that day.

I saw the branches of the trees
    Bend down thy touch to meet,
The clover-blossoms in the grass
    Rise up to kiss thy feet.

"Sleep, sleep to-day, tormenting cares,
    Of earth and folly born!"
Solemnly sang the village choir
    On that sweet Sabbath morn.

Through the closed blinds the golden sun
    Poured in a dusty beam,
Like the celestial ladder seen
    By Jacob in his dream.

And ever and anon the wind,
    Sweet-scented with the hay,
Turned o'er the hymn-book's fluttering leaves
    That on the window lay.

Long was the good man's sermon,
    Yet it seemed not so to me;
For he spake of Ruth the beautiful,
    And still I thought of thee.

Long was the prayer he uttered,
  Yet it seemed not so to me;
For in my heart I prayed with him,
  And still I thought of thee.

But now, alas! the place seems changed;
  Thou art no longer here:
Part of the sunshine of the scene
  With thee did disappear.

Though thoughts, deep-rooted in my heart,
  Like pine-trees dark and high,
Subdue the light of noon, and breathe
  A low and ceaseless sigh.

This memory brightens o'er the past,
  As when the sun, concealed
Behind some cloud that near us hangs,
  Shines on a distant field.

LONGFELLOW

THE SABBATH BELL.

THE Sabbath bell! the Sabbath bell!
  To toil-worn men a soothing sound;
Now labor rests beneath its spell,
  And holy stillness reigns around:

The ploughman's team, the thresher's flail,
   The woodman's axe, their clamors cease,
And only nature's notes prevail,
   To humble bosoms echoing peace.

The Sabbath bell! the Sabbath bell!
   How sweet on ears devout it falls,
While its sweet chime, with varying swell,
   The rich and poor to worship calls.
Hark! hark! again with sharper peals
   It chides the laggard's fond delay;
Now through the vale it softly steals,
   To cheer the timely on their way.

The Sabbath bell! the Sabbath bell!
   What soul-awakening sounds we hear!
Its blessed invitations tell
   Of welcome to the house of prayer.
"Come, sinner, come," it seems to cry;
   "Oh! never doubt thy Maker's love;
Christ has thy ransom paid, then why
   Delay his clemency to prove?"

The Sabbath bell! the Sabbath bell!
   Oft have we heard its warning chime,

And yet we love the world too well,
　Nor feel our waywardness a crime:
Yet still thy calls, sweet bell, repeat,
　Till, ended all our mortal strife,
In hand-built shrines no more we meet,
　But worship in the realms of life.

The Sabbath bell! the Sabbath bell!
　Its friendly summons peals no more;
The thronging crowds pour in with zeal
　The Great Jehovah to adore.
Hence! fancy wild, hence! earth-born care;
　With awe let hallowed courts be trod;
Wake all the soul to love and prayer,
　And reverence the present God!

Anon.

SUNDAY.

Thou blessed day! I will not call thee last,
　Nor Sabbath,—last nor first of all the seven,
　But a calm slip of intervening heaven,
Between the uncertain future and the past;
As in a stormy night, amid the blast,

Comes ever and anon a truce on high,
And a calm lake of pure and starry sky
Peers through the mountainous depths of clouds
    amassed.
Sweet day of prayer! e'en they whose scrupulous
    dread
Will call no other day as others do,
Might call thee Sunday without fear or blame!
For thy bright morn delivered from the dead
    Our Sun of Life, and will for aye renew
To faithful souls the import of thy name.
HARTLEY COLERIDGE.

SUNDAY.

THE Sabbath-day, of every day the best,
The poor man's happiness, a poor man sings;
When labor has no claim to break his rest,
And the light hours fly swift on easy wings.
What happiness this holy morning brings,
How soft its pleasures on his senses steal;
How sweet the village-bells' first warning rings;

And oh! how comfortable does he feel,
When with his family at ease he takes his early
   meal.

The careful wife displays her frugal hoard,
And both partake in comfort, though they're
   poor;
While love's sweet offsprings crowd the lowly
   board,
Their little likenesses in miniature.
Though through the week he labor does endure,
And weary limbs oft cause him to complain,
This welcome morning always brings a cure;
It teems with joys his soul to entertain,
And doubly sweet appears the pleasure after pain.

Ah, who can tell the bliss, from labor freed,
His leisure meeteth on a Sunday morn,
Fixed in a chair, some godly book to read,
Or wandering round to view the crops of corn,
In best clothes fitted out, and beard new shorn;
Dropping adown in some warm sheltered dell,
With six days' labor weak and weary worn;
List'ning around each distant chiming bell,
That on the soft'ning breeze melodiously doth swell.

And oft he takes his family abroad
In short excursions o'er the field and plain,
Marking each little object on his road,
An insect, sprig of grass, and ear of grain;
Endeavoring thus most simply to maintain
That the same Power that bids the mite to crawl,
That browns the wheat-lands in their summer-stain,
That Power which formed the simple flower withal,
Formed all that lives and grows upon this earthly ball.

* * * *

Hail, sacred Sabbath! hail, thou poor man's joy!
Thou oft hast been a comfort to my care,
When faint and weary with the week's employ,
I met thy presence in my corner-chair,
Musing and bearing up with troubles there;
Thrice hail, thou heavenly boon! by God's decree
At first creation planned, that all might share,
Both man and beast, some hours from labor free,
To offer thanks to Him whose mercy sent us thee.

This day the field a sweeter clothing wears,
A Sunday scene looks brighter to the eye;

SUNDAY.

And hast'ning on to Monday morning's cares,
With double speed the winged hour gallops by.
How swift the sun streaks down the western sky,
Scarcely perceived till it begins to wane,
When ploughboys mark his setting with a sigh,
Dreading the morn's approaching hours with pain,
When capon's restless calls awake to toil again.

As the day closes on its peace and rest,
The godly man sits down and takes "the Book,"
To close it in a manner deemed the best;
And for a suiting chapter doth he look,
That may for comfort and a guide be took:
He reads of patient Job, his trials' thrall,
How men are troubled when by God forsook,
And prays with David to bear up with all;—
When sleep shuts up the scene, soft as the night-dews fall.

CLARE.

THE VOICE OF PRAYER.

I hear it in the summer wind,
   I feel it in the lightning's gleam;
A tongue in every leaf I find,
   A voice in every running stream.
It speaks in the enamelled flower,
   With grateful incense borne on high;
It echoes in the dripping shower,
   And breathes in midnight's breathless sky.
Through all her scenes of foul and fair,
Nature presents a fervent prayer;
In all her myriad shapes of love,
Nature transmits a prayer above.

Day unto day, and night to night,
   The eloquent appeal convey;
Flasheth the cheerful orb of light,
   To bid creation bend and pray:
The shadowy clouds of darkness steal
   Along the horizon's azure cope,
Bidding distracted nations kneel
   To Him, the Lord of quenchless hope;

THE VOICE OF PRAYER.

To Him, who died that hope might live,
And lived, eternal life to give;
Who bore the pangs of death, to save
The dead from an eternal grave.

Oh! thread you tangled coppice now,
    Where the sweetbrier and woodbine strive,
Where music drops from every bough,
    Like honey from the forest hive;
Where warbling birds, and humming bees,
    And wild-flowers round a gushing spring,
And blossoms sprinkled o'er the trees,
    And gorgeous insects on the wing,
Unite to load the gladdened air
With melody of grateful prayer;
Unite their Maker's name to bless
In that brief span of happiness!

And can it be that man alone
    Forbids the tide of prayer to flow,
For whom his God forsook a throne,
    To weep, to bleed—a man of woe?
Ah! 'tis *alone* the immortal soul,
    An endless bliss ordained to win,

The heaven of heavens its destined goal,
That thus is sunk in shameless sin?
Scantly permitting to intrude
The faintest gleam of gratitude;
And but in hours of dire despair,
Responding in the voice of prayer!

ANON

THE LORD'S DAY.

Hail to the day, which He, who made the heaven,
Earth, and their armies, sanctified and blest,
Perpetual memory of the Maker's rest!
Hail to the day, when He, by whom was given
New life to man, the tomb asunder riven,
Arose! That day his Church hath still confest,
At once Creation's and Redemption's feast,
Sign of a world called forth, a world forgiven.
Welcome that day, the day of holy peace,
The Lord's own day! to man's Creator owed,
And man's Redeemer; for the soul's increase
In sanctity, and sweet repose bestowed;
Type of the rest when sin and care shall cease,
The rest remaining for the oved of God!

Bp MANT

THERE IS A TONGUE IN EVERY LEAF

There is a tongue in every leaf!
   A voice in every rill!
A voice that speaketh everywhere,
In flood and fire, through earth and air;
   A tongue that's never still!

'Tis the Great Spirit wide diffused
   Through everything we see,
That with our spirits communeth
Of things mysterious—Life and Death,
   Time and Eternity.

I see him in the blazing sun,
   And in the thunder-cloud;
I hear Him in the mighty roar
That rusheth through the forests hoar,
   When winds are raging loud.

I feel Him in the silent dews,
   By grateful earth betrayed;
I feel Him in the gentle showers,
The soft south wind, the breath of flowers,
   The sunshine, and the shade.

I see Him, hear Him, everywhere,
  In all things—darkness, light;
Silence, and sound; but most of all,
 When slumber's dusky curtains fall,
  I' the silent hour of night.

ANON.

A SUNDAY THOUGHT.

How calm the quiet, sweet the rest,
  That breathes at such a time!
How dear to every pious breast
  The church-bells' soothing chime!

A day of prayer, of holy thought,
  And blessed peace it is;
And did we keep it as we ought,
  A day of sacred bliss.

How welcome then of all the seven
  This day would be allowed:
A foretaste of the joys of heaven,
  A passport to our God.

ANON.

A DOMESTIC SCENE.

'Twas early day—and sunlight streamed
   Soft through a quiet room,
That hushed, but not forsaken seemed—
   Still, but with nought of gloom,
For then, secure in happy age,
   Whose hope is from above,
A father communed with the page
   Of Heaven's recorded love.

Pure fell the beam and meekly bright,
   On his gray holy hair,
And touched the book with tenderest light,
   As if its shrine were there;
But oh! that patriarch's aspect shone
   With something lovelier far—
A radiance, all the Spirits own,
   Caught not from sun or star.

Some word of life e'en then had met
   His calm benignant eye,
Some ancient promise, breathing yet
   Of immortality;

Some heart's deep language, when the glow
  Of quenchless faith survives,
For, every feature said—"I know
  That my Redeemer lives."

And silent stood his children by,
  Hushing their very breath,
Before the solemn sanctity
  Of thought, o'er-sweeping death;
Silent—yet did not each young breast
  With love and reverence melt?
Oh! blest be those fair girls—and blest
  That home where God is felt.

HEMANS

THE SABBATH BELLS.

THE cheerful Sabbath bells, wherever heard,
Strike pleasant on the sense, most like the voice
Of one who, from the far-off hills, proclaims
Tidings of good to Zion: chiefly when
Their piercing tones fall sudden on the ear
Of the contemplant solitary man,
Whom thoughts abstruse or high have chanced to lure.

Forth from the walks of men revolving oft,
And oft again, hard matter which eludes
And baffles his pursuit,—thought-sick and tired
Of controversy, where no end appears,
No clue to his research, the lonely man
Half wishes for society again.
Him, thus engaged, the Sabbath bells salute,
Sudden! his heart awakes, his ears drink in
The cheering music; his relenting soul
Yearns after all the joys of social life,
And softens with the love of human kind.

CHARLES LAMB

THE SABBATH ON THE SEAS.

'T<small>IS</small> sweet to hear the Sabbath bells
Ring out on woodlands, floods, and fells;
Now clear and jubilant, anon
Mellowed and mournful they chime on.
And sweet from church or chapel reared,
Midst glens, to rural hearts endeared,
Oh, sweetly, on the morning air,
Sounds the meek hymn ascending there,

THE SABBATH ON THE SEAS.

When rural voices join to raise
An anthem to their Maker's praise!

And solemn and majestic floats,
The organ-chant in rolling notes,
Poured richly down the pillared aisle
Of some time-hallowed Gothic pile.
When mingle then in prayer and song,
A city's thousand voices strong;
Oh, who unmoved can listen then
To the responsive deep amen?
The soft refulgent light that streams
Through windows mapped with holiest themes,
The blazonry of cherub wings,
Proclaim Thy temple, King of kings!
And marbled tablets, sculptured round,
Mark where the dead have refuge found.
Such are the Sabbath-notes that rise
From earth's vast altar to the skies;
And have the ocean-waves no voice
To bid the sacred hours rejoice?
Have they, who on the dangerous deep
For life an anxious vigil keep,

No tribute for the Almighty One,
Who rules them from his viewless throne?
Hark! o'er the wide and bellowing main
Soft music comes, a choral strain.
And, kneeling on the barrier frail,
(How vain their strength if that should fail!)
That lifts them from the yawning sea,
   Bold rugged men are grouped in prayer,
In childlike pure simplicity,
   And, lo! their God is with them there.

Godwin

THE SABBATH EVE.

Is there a time when moments flow
   More lovelily than all beside,
It is, of all the times below,
   A Sabbath Eve in summer-tide.

Oh! then the setting sun smiles fair,
   And all below and all above,
The different forms of nature, wear
   One universal garb of love.

THE SABBATH EVE.

And then the peace that Jesus beams,
    The life of grace, the death of sin,
With nature's placid woods and streams,
    Is peace without, and peace within.

Delightful scene—a world at rest.
    A God all love—no grief, no fear,
A heavenly hope—a peaceful breast,
    A smile unsullied by a tear.

If heaven be ever felt below,
    A scene so heavenly sure as this
May cause a heart on earth to know
    Some foretaste of celestial bliss.

Delightful hour—how soon will night
    Spread her dark mantle o'er thy reign,
And morrow's quick returning light
    Must call us to the world again.

Yet will there dawn at last a day,
    A sun that never sets shall rise;
Night will not veil a ceaseless ray!
    The heavenly Sabbath never dies!

                                            ANON.

THE SAILOR'S EVENING PRAYER

Long the sun hath gone to rest,
Dimmed is now the deepening west;
And the sky hath lost the hue
That the rich clouds o'er it threw:
Lonely on the pale-blue sky
Gleam faint streaks of crimson dye,
Gloriously the evening star
Looks upon us from afar;
Aid us, o'er the changeful deep,
 God of Power;
Bless the sailor's ocean-sleep
 At midnight's hour.

On the stilly twilight air
We would breathe our solemn prayer,—
"Bless the dear ones of our home,
Guide us through the wild wave's foam,
To the light of those dear eyes,
Where our heart's best treasure lies,
To the love in *one* fond breast;
That unchanging home of rest!

Hear her, when at even-tide
  She kneels to pray,
That God would bless, defend, and guide
  Those far away!"

Now the moon hath touched the sea,
And the waves, all tremblingly,
Throw towards heaven their silvery spray,
Happy in the gladdening ray:
Thus, Redeemer, let thy love
Shine upon us from above;
Touched by Thee, our hearts will rise,
Grateful towards the glowing skies;
Guard us, shield us, mighty Lord,
  Thou dost not sleep;
Still the tempest with thy word,—
  Rule the deep!

ANON.

THE FIRST SABBATH.

SIX days the heavenly host, in circle vast,
Like that untouching cincture which enzones
The globe of Saturn, compassed wide this orb,
And with the forming mass floated along,

In rapid course, through yet untravelled space,
Beholding God's stupendous power,—a world
Bursting from chaos at the omnific will,
And perfect ere the sixth day's evening star
On Paradise arose. Blessed that eve!
The Sabbath's harbinger, when, all complete,
In freshest beauty from Jehovah's hand,
Creation bloomed; when Eden's twilight face
Smiled like a sleeping babe: the voice divine
A holy calm breathed o'er the goodly work:
Mildly the sun upon the loftiest trees,
Shed mellowly a sloping beam. Peace reigned,
And love, and gratitude; the human pair
Their orisons poured forth; love, concord, reigned,
The falcon, perched upon the blooming bough
With Philomela, listened to her lay;
Among the antlered herd, the tiger couched
Harmless; the lion's mane no terror spread
Among the careless ruminating flock.
Silence was o'er the deep; the noiseless surge,
The last subsiding wave,—of that dread tumult
Which raged, when Ocean, at the mute command,
Rushed furiously into his new-cleft bed,—
Was gently rippling on the pebbled shore;

While, on the swell, the sea-bird with her head
Wing-veiled, slept tranquilly. The host of heaven,
Entranced in new delight, speechless adored;
Nor stopped their fleet career, nor changed their form
Encircular, till on that hemisphere,—
In which the blissful garden sweet exhaled
Its incense, odorous clouds,—the Sabbath dawn
Arose; then wide the flying circle oped,
And soared, in semblance of a mighty rainbow.
Silent ascend the choirs of Seraphim;
No harp resounds, mute is each voice; the burst
Of joy and praise, reluctant they repress,—
For love and concord all things so attuned
To harmony, that Earth must have received
The grand vibration, and to the centre shook:
But soon as to the starry altitudes
They reached, then what a storm of sound, tremendous,
Swelled through the realms of space! The morning stars
Together sang, and all the sons of God
Shouted for joy! Loud was the peal; so loud
As would have quite o'erwhelmed human sense;

But to the earth it came a gentle strain,
Like softest fall breathed from Æolian lute,
When 'mid the cords the evening gale expires.
Day of the Lord! creation's hallowed close!
Day of the Lord! (prophetical they sang)
Benignant mitigation of that doom,
Which must, ere long, consign the fallen race,
Dwellers in yonder star, to toil and woe!
                                                    GRAHAME.

A WINTER SABBATH WALK.

How dazzling white the snowy scene! deep, deep,
The stillness of the winter Sabbath day,—
Not even a footfall heard. Smooth are the fields,
Each hollow pathway level with the plain:
Hid are the bushes, save that, here and there,
Are seen the topmost shoots of brier or broom.
High-ridged, the whirled drift has almost reached
The powdered keystone of the churchyard porch.
Mute hangs the hooded bell; the tombs lie buried;
No step approaches to the house of prayer,

 The flickering fall is o'er; the clouds disperse,
And show the sun, hung o'er the welkin's verge,

Shooting a bright but ineffectual beam
On all the sparkling waste. Now is the time
To visit nature in her grand attire;
Though perilous the mountainous ascent,
A noble recompense the danger brings.
How beautiful the plain stretched far below!
Unvaried though it be, save by yon stream
With azure windings, or the leafless wood.
But what the beauty of the plain, compared
To that sublimity which reigns enthroned,
Holding joint rule with solitude divine,
Among yon rocky fells, that bid defiance
To steps the most adventurously bold!
There silence dwells profound; or if the cry
Of high-poised eagle break at times the calm,
The mantled echoes no response return.

But let me now explore the deep-sunk dell.
No footprint, save the covey's or the flock's,
Is seen along the rill, where marshy springs
Still rear the grassy blade of vivid green.
Beware, ye shepherds, of these treacherous haunts,
Nor linger there too long: the wintry day
Soon closes; and full oft a heavier fall,

Heaped by the blast, fills up the sheltered glen,
While, gurgling deep below, the buried rill
Mines for itself a snow-coved way. Oh! then,
Your helpless charge drive from the tempting spot,
And keep them on the bleak hill's stormy side,
Where night-winds sweep the gathering drift away:
So the great Shepherd leads the heavenly flock
From faithless pleasures, full into the storms
Of life, where long they bear the bitter blast,
Until at length the vernal sun looks forth,
Bedimmed with showers: then to the pastures green
He brings them, where the quiet waters glide,
The streams of life, the Siloah of the soul.

GRAHAME

* * * * * *

THE night was winter in his roughest mood;
The morning sharp and clear. But now at noon,
Upon the southern side of the slant hills,
And where the woods fence off the northern blast,
The season smiles, resigning all its rage,
And has the warmth of May. The vault is blue
Without a cloud, and white without a speck
The dazzling splendor of the scene below.

A WINTER SABBATH WALK.

Again the harmony comes o'er the vale;
And through the trees I view the embattled tower,
Whence all the music. I again perceive
The soothing influence of the wafted strains,
And settle in soft musings as I tread
The walk, still verdant, under oaks and elms,
Whose outspread branches overarch the glade.
The roof, though movable through all its length
As the wind sways it, has yet well sufficed,
And, intercepting in their silent fall
The frequent flakes, has kept a path for me.
No noise is here, or none that hinders thought
The redbreast warbles still, but is content
With slender notes, and more than half suppressed;
Pleased with his solitude, and flitting light
From spray to spray, where'er he rests he shakes
From many a twig the pendent drops of ice,
That tinkle in the withered leaves below.
Stillness, accompanied with sounds so soft,
Charms more than silence

COWPER.

EARLY RISING AND PRAYER.

When first thy eyes unveil, give thy soul leave
    To do the like; our bodies but forerun
The spirit's duty; true hearts spread and heave
    Unto their God, as flowers do to the sun:
Give Him thy first thoughts then, so shalt thou keep
Him company all day, and in Him sleep.

Yet never sleep the sun up; prayer should
    Dawn with the day: these are set awful hours
'Twixt heaven and us; the manna was not good
    After sunrising; for day sullies flowers:
Rise to prevent the sun; sleep doth sins glut,
And heaven's gates open when the world is shut.

Walk with thy fellow-creatures; note the hush
    And whisperings amongst them. Not a spring
Or leaf but hath his morning hymn; each bush
    And oak doth know I AM!—Canst thou not sing?
Oh! leave thy cares and follies! go this way,
And thou art sure to prosper all the day.

EARLY RISING AND PRAYER.

Serve God before the world; let Him not go
    Until thou hast a blessing; then resign
The whole unto Him, and remember who
    Prevailed by wrestling ere the sun did shine:
Pour oil upon the stones, seek sin forgiven,
Then journey on, and have an eye to heaven.

Mornings are mysteries: the first world's youth,
    Man's resurrection, and the future's bud,
Shroud in their births; the crown of life, light, truth,
    Is styled their star; the stone and hidden food:
Three blessings wait upon them, one of which
Should move—they make us holy, happy, rich.

When the world's up, and every swarm abroad,
    Keep well thy temper, mix not with each clay;
Despatch necessities; life hath a load
    Which must be carried on, and safely may:
Yet keep those cares without thee; let the heart
Be God's alone, and choose the better part.

VAUGHAN.

THE SABBATH.

It is not only in the sacred fane
That homage should be paid to the Most High;
There is a temple, one not made with hands,—
The vaulted firmament: far in the woods,
Almost beyond the sound of city-chime,
At intervals heard through the breezeless air;
When not the limberest leaf is seen to move,
Save where the linnet lights upon the spray;
When not a floweret bends its little stalk,
Save where the bee alights upon the bloom;—
There, rapt in gratitude, in joy, and love,
The man of God will pass the Sabbath noon;
Silence his praise: his disembodied thoughts,
Loosed from the load of words, will high ascend
Beyond the empyrean.–
Nor yet less pleasing at the heavenly throne,
The Sabbath service of the shepherd boy.
In some lone glen, where every sound is lulled
To slumber, save the tinkling of the rill,
Or bleat of lamb, or hovering falcon's cry,
Stretched on the sward, he reads of Jesse's son;

Or sheds a tear o'er him to Egypt sold,
And wonders why he weeps: the volume closed,
With thyme-sprig laid between the leaves, he sings
The sacred lays, his weekly lesson, conned
With meikle care beneath the lowly roof
Where humble lore is learnt, where humble worth
Pines unrewarded by a thankless state.
Thus reading, hymning, all alone, unseen,
The shepherd boy the Sabbath holy keeps,
Till on the heights he marks the straggling bands
Returning homeward from the house of prayer.
In peace they home resort. O blissful days!
When all men worship God as conscience wills.

GRAHAME.

THE BEAUTIES OF NATURE.

It was a lovely morning;—all was calm,
  As if creation, thankful for repose,
In renovated beauty, breathing balm
    And blessedness around, from slumber rose,
  Joyful once more to see the East unclose
Its gates of glory:—yet subdued and mild,
  Like the soft smile of patience amid woes

By hope and resignation reconciled,
That morning's beauty shone, that landscape's charm
    beguiled.

The heavens were marked by many a filmy streak
    Even in the orient; and the sun shone through
Those lines, as Hope upon a mourner's cheek
    Sheds, meekly chastened, her delightful hue.
    From groves and meadows, all impearled with
        dew,
Rose silvery mists,—no eddying winds swept by,—
    The cottage chimneys, half concealed from view
By their embowering foliage, sent on high
Their pallid wreaths of smoke unruffled to the sky.

And every gentle sound which broke the hush
    Of morning's still serenity was sweet:
The skylark overhead; the speckled thrush,
    Who now had taken with delight his seat
    Upon the slender larch, the day to greet;
The starling chattering to her callow young;
    And that monotonous lay, which seems to fleet
Like echo through the air, the cuckoo's song,
Was heard at times, far off, the leafy woods among.

Surrounded by such sights and sounds, I stood
  Delighted auditor, spectator here ;
And gave full scope, in meditative mood,
  To thoughts excited by a scene so fair ;
Feeling renewedly how matchless are
The power and goodness of that Great Supreme
  Who formed and fashioned all things to declare
Even to those who lightly of Him deem,
The beauty and the love of his creative scheme.

BARTON.

THE COVENANTER'S SABBATH.

'Twas Sabbath morn, a lovelier never rose,
And nature seemed in holy, calm repose ;
No cloud was seen along the azure sky,
And the pure streamlet glided softly by ;
From tree to tree the warbling minstrels sung,
And heaven's bright arch with nature's praises
    rung ;
Though all was still, yet persecution's rage,
With awful fury scourged a bleeding age ;
Then Scotland groaned beneath a tyrant's yoke,
Till her proud spirit seemed for ever broke ;

Her sons were hunted from the abodes of men,
To savage wilds, or some sequestered glen:
Justice stood mute, for demons gave the law,
And many a bloody scene her mountains saw.
What though this morning rose so calmly bright,
The eye which saw it trembled at its light;
On Loudon's braes the bird might find a nest;
On Pentland's hills the wounded deer might rest;
But terror there her gloomy watch did keep,
Like the death-storm which overhangs the deep;
And homeless man from place to place was driven,
Bereft of hope, and every stay but heaven.
No gladsome bell announced the Sabbath day,
The solemn temples mouldered with decay;
God's people met, amidst the lonely wild,
Like wretched outcasts from a world exiled;
In a lone cave, the eagle's drear abode,
They met to worship and to praise their God;
The fretted rocks around their temple hung,
And echoed back the praises as they sung;
Though half suppressed the thrilling accents rise,
To God who hears and answers in the skies;
The preacher rose, and every voice grew still,
Save echoing breezes round the lonely hill;

With solemn awe he opes the blessed Book,
Earnest in voice, and heavenly in his look;
While from his lips the soothing accents flow,
To cheer his flock and mitigate their woe;
For who could tell how soon the sentinel's breath
Might give the signal of approaching death;
For every moment seemed to them the last,
And days to come, more gloomy than the past.

Within that place, the sacramental board
Was spread in memory of their risen Lord,
While the deep thunder rent the thick'ning cloud
And lightning flashed along the mournful crowd;
And when with lowly hands the bread was broke,
The sflected flame fell on the living rock;
Illumed the table with its symbols spread,
As if heaven's brightness rested on their head.
With placid looks they saw the darkening cloud,
Which hid Jehovah in his awful shroud;
And when the voice fell deafening on the ear,
No murmuring word proclaim them men of fear,
But calm and sweet the heaven-tuned "Martyrs'
  rose
Like zephyrs sighing at the tempest's close.

Near to this place where mountain torrents flow
Through broken rocks, to calmer scenes below,
How oft was heard the tender infant's sigh,
Its name pronounced midst breezes passing by;
While all unconscious of the holy rite,
It smiled amidst the dangers of the night.
In caves and glens their Sabbath hours were spent,
Till the pale moon illumed the firmament;
And there they wandered at the dead of night,
When the dim stars withheld their glimmering light;
And, oh, how oft their wild retreat's been found
By those who sought them like the blood-trained hound,
And made that place, their oft frequented cave,
The holy martyr's solitary grave;
When nought but winds their dreary death-knell rung,
And the scared bird their mournful requiem sung!
Yet heaven wept, and bade their spirits rise
On angel wings, from sorrow to the skies;
While all they suffered shall be ne'er forgot,
Their grave be hallowed, and their dying spot;

For they to Scotland gave her church, her laws,
And fell like patriots in their country's cause.
Peace to their memory! let no impious breath
Soil their fair fame, or triumph o'er their death;
Let Scotia's grateful sons their tear-drops shed,
Where low they lie in honor's gory bed;
Rich with the spoils their glorious deeds had won,
And purchased freedom to a land undone;
A land which owes its glory and its worth
To those whom tyrants banished from the earth.

WEIR

A SABBATH MEDITATION.

With silent awe I hail the sacred morn,
   That slowly wakes while all the fields are still;
A soothing calm on every breeze is borne,
   A graver murmur gurgles from the rill,
   And echo answers softer from the hill,
And softer sings the linnet from the thorn;
   The skylark warbles in a tone less shrill.
Hail, light serene! hail, sacred Sabbath morn!
   The rooks float silently, in airy drove;

The sun a placid yellow lustre throws;
  The gales, that lately sighed along the grove,
Have hushed their downy wings in dead repose;
  The hovering rack of clouds forgets to move:—
So smiled the day when the first morn arose.
LEYDEN.

SABBATH EVENING.

ANOTHER day has passed along,
  And we are nearer to the tomb!
Nearer to join the heavenly song,
  Or hear the last eternal doom.

These moments of departing day,
  When thought is calm, and labors cease,
Are surely solemn times to pray,
  To ask for pardon and for peace.

Thou God of mercy, swift to hear,
  More swift than man to tell his need;
Be Thou to us this evening near,
  And to Thy fount our spirits lead.

Teach us to pray—and, having taught,
  Grant us the blessings that we crave;

SABBATH EVENING.

Without Thy teaching—prayer is nought;
    But with it—powerful to save!

Sweet is the light of Sabbath Eve,
    And soft the sunbeam lingering there;
Those sacred hours this low earth leave,
    Wafted on wings of praise and prayer.

This time, how lovely and how still!
    Peace shines, and smiles on all below;
The plain, the stream, the wood, the hill,
    All fair with evening's setting glow!

Season of Rest! the tranquil soul
    Feels thy sweet calm, and melts in love:
And while these sacred moments roll,
    Faith sees a smiling heaven above.

How short the time, how soon the sun
    Sets! and dark night resumes her reign!
And soon the hours of rest are done,
    Then morrow brings the world again.

Yet will our journey not be long,
    Our pilgrimage will soon be trod;
And we shall join the ceaseless song,
    The endless Sabbath of our God.

                      EDMESTON.

SABBATH WALKS.

Upon the Sabbath, sweet it is to walk
'Neath woodside shelter of oak's spreading tree,
Or by a hedge-row track, or padded balk;
Or stretch 'neath willows on the meadow lea,
List'ning, delighted, hum of passing bee,
And curious pausing on the blossom's head;
   And mark the spider at his labor free,
Spinning from bent to bent his silken thread;
   And lab'ring ants, by careful nature led
To make the most of summer's plenteous stay;
   And lady-cow, beneath its leafy shed,
Called, when I mixed with children, "clock-a-clay,"
   Pruning its red wings on its pleasing bed,
Glad like myself to shun the heat of day.

CLARE.

How sweet the tuneful bells' responsive peal!
As when, at opening morn, the fragrant breeze
Breathes on the trembling sense of wan disease,
So piercing to my heart their force I feel!
And hark! with lessening cadence now they fall,
And now, along the white and level tide,
They fling their melancholy music wide;
Bidding me many a tender thought recall
Of summer days, and those delightful years
When by my native streams, in life's fair prime,
The mournful magic of their mingling chime
First waked my wondering childhood into tears!
But seeming now, when all those days are o'er,
The sounds of joy once heard, and heard no more.

POWLES.

WAR.

* * * *

Of all the murderous trades by mortals plied,
'Tis War alone that never violates
The hallowed day by simulate respect,—
By hypocritic rest: No, no, the work proceeds,
From sacred pinnacles are hung the flags,
That give the sign to slip the leash from slaughter.
The bells, whose knoll a holy calmness poured
Into the good man's breast,—whose sound solaced
The sick, the poor, the old—perversion dire—
Pealing with sulphurous tongue, speak death-fraught
    words:
From morn to eve Destruction revels frenzied,
Till at the hour when peaceful vesper-chimes
Were wont to soothe the ear, the trumpet sounds
Pursuit and flight altern; and for the song
Of larks, descending to their grass-bowered homes,
The croak of flesh-gorged ravens, as they slake
Their thirst in hoof-prints filled with gore, disturbs
The stupor of the dying man; while Death
Triumphantly sails down the ensanguined stream,
On corses throned, and crowned with shivered
    boughs,
That erst hung imaged in the crystal tide.

GRAHAME.

SUNDAYS.

Bright shadows of true rest! some shoots of bliss!
   Heaven once a week;
The next world's gladness prepossessed in this;
   A day to seek
Eternity in time; the steps by which
   We climb above all ages; lamps that light
Man through his heap of dark days; and the rich
   And full redemption of the whole week's flight:
The pulleys unto headlong man; time's bower;
   The narrow way;
Transplanted paradise; God's walking hour;
   The cool o' the day;
The creature's jubilee; God's parle with dust;
   Heaven here; man on those hills of myrrh, of
     flowers;
Angels descending; the returns of trust;
   A gleam of glory after six days' showers;
The Church's love-feasts: time's prerogative
   And interest
Deducted from the whole; the combs and hive,
   And home of rest;

The Milky Way chalked out with suns; a clue
  That guides through erring hours, and in full
    story;
A taste of heaven on earth; the pledge and cue
  Of a full feast, and the out-courts of glory.
                                        VAUGHAN.

THE SABBATH.

Lord of the Sabbath and its light!
  I hail Thy hallowed day of rest;
It is my weary soul's delight,
  The solace of my care-worn breast.

Its dewy morn—its glowing noon—
  Its tranquil eve—its solemn night—
Pass sweetly; but they pass too soon,
  And leave me saddened at their flight.

Yet sweetly as they glide along,
  And hallowed though the calm they yield;
Transporting though their rapt'rous song,
  And heav'nly visions seem reveale l:

My soul is desolate and drear,
  My silent harp untuned remains,
Unless, my Saviour, Thou art near,
  To heal my wounds and soothe my pains.

O ever, ever let me hail
  Thy presence with Thy day of rest!
Then will Thy servant never fail
  To deem Thy Sabbaths doubly blest.

EAST.

AN EVENING HYMN.

How many days, with mute adieu,
  Have gone down yon untrodden sky!
And still it looks as clear and blue
  As when it first was hung on high.
The rolling sun, the frowning cloud
  That drew the lightning in its rear,
The thunder, tramping deep and loud,
  Have left no footmark there.

The village bells, with silver chime,
  Come softened by the distant shore;

AN EVENING HYMN.

Though I have heard them many a time,
    They never rung so sweet before.
A silence rests upon the hill,
    A listening awe pervades the air:
The very flowers are shut, and still,
    And bowed as if in prayer.

And in this hushed and breathless close,
    O'er earth, and air, and sky, and sea,
That still low voice in silence goes,
    Which speaks alone, great God! of Thee
The whispering leaves, the far-off brook,
    The linnet's warble fainter grown,
The hive-bound bee, the lonely rook,—
    All these their Maker own.

Now shine the starry hosts of light,
    Gazing on earth with golden eyes;
Bright guardians of the blue-browed night!
    What are ye in your native skies?
I know not! neither can I know,
    Nor on what leader ye attend,
Nor whence ye came, nor whither go,
    Nor what your aim or end.

AN EVENING HYMN.

I know they must be holy things
    That from a roof so sacred shine,
Where sounds the beat of angel-wings,
    And footsteps echo all Divine.
Their mysteries I never sought,
    Nor hearkened to what Science tells,
For oh! in childhood I was taught
    That God amidst them dwells.

The darkening woods, the fading trees,
    The grasshopper's last feeble sound,
The flowers just wakened by the breeze,
    All leave the stillness more profound.
The twilight takes a deeper shade,
    The dusky pathways blacker grow,
And silence reigns in glen and glade,—
    All, all is mute below.

And other eves as sweet as this
    Will close upon as calm a day,
And, sinking down the deep abyss,
    Will, like the last, be swept away;
Until eternity is gained,
    That boundless sea without a shore,

That without time for ever reigned,
    And will when time's no more.

Now nature sinks in soft repose,
    A living semblance of the grave;
The dew steals noiseless on the rose,
    The boughs have almost ceased to wave;
The silent sky, the sleeping earth,
    Tree, mountain, stream, the humble sod,
All tell from whom they had their birth,
    And cry, "Behold a God!"

THOMAS MILLER.

THE TIME FOR PRAYER.

When is the time for prayer?—
With the first beams that light the morning sky,
Ere for the toils of day thou dost prepare,
    Lift up thy thoughts on high;
Commend thy loved ones to His watchful care!—
    Morn is the time for prayer!

And in the noontide hour,
If worn by toil or by sad cares opprest,
Then unto God thy spirit's sorrow pour,
    And He will give thee rest:—
Thy voice shall reach Him through the fields of air :
    Noon is the time for prayer!

When the bright sun hath set,—
Whilst yet eve's glowing colors deck the skies;—
When with the loved, at home, again thou'st met,
    Then let thy prayer arise
For those who in thy joys and sorrows share :—
    Eve is the time for prayer!

And when the stars come forth,—
When to the trusting heart sweet hopes are given,
And the deep stillness of the hour gives birth
 To pure bright dreams of heaven,—
Kneel to thy God; ask strength, life's ills to bear:
 Night is the time for prayer!

 When is the time for prayer?
In every hour, while life is spared to thee—
In crowds or solitude—in joy or care—
 Thy thoughts should heavenward flee.
At home—at morn and eve—with loved ones there,
 Bend thou the knee in prayer!

Anon.

SOCIAL WORSHIP.

There is a joy, which angels well may prize:
 To see, and hear, and aid God's worship, when
 Unnumbered tongues, a host of Christian men,
Youths, matrons, maidens, join. Their sounds arise,
"Like many waters;" now glad symphonies
 Of thanks and glory to our God; and then,
 Seal of the social prayer, the loud Amen,
Faith's common pledge, contrition's mingled cries.

Thus when the Church of Christ was hale and
    young,
She called on God, one spirit and one voice;
Thus from corruption cleansed, with health new
    strung,
Her sons she nurtured. Oh! be theirs, by choice,
What duty bids, to worship, heart and tongue;
At once to pray, at once in God rejoice!

Bp. MANT.

THE CURFEW BELL.

I.

SOLEMNLY, mournfully,
    Dealing its dole,
The curfew bell
    Is beginning to toll:

Cover the embers,
    And put out the light;
Toil comes with the morning,
    And rest with the night.

Dark grow the windows,
    And quenched is the fire;
Sound fades into silence,—
    All footsteps retire.

THE CURFEW BELL.

No voice in the chambers,
   No sound in the hall;
Sleep and oblivion
   Reign over all!

II.

The book is completed,
   And, closed, like the day;
And the hand that has written it
   Lays it away.

Dim grow its fancies;
   Forgotten they lie;
Like coals in the ashes,
   They darken and die.

Song sinks into silence,
   The story is told,
The windows are darkened,
   The hearthstone is cold.

Darker and darker
   The black shadows fall;
Sleep and oblivion
   Reign over all.

                          LONGFELLOW.

THE SABBATH.

On the seventh day reposing, lo! the great Creator stood,
Saw the glorious work accomplished,—saw and felt that it was good;
Heaven, earth, man and beast have being, day and night their courses run,—
First creation,—infant manhood,—earliest Sabbath,—it is done.

On the seventh day reposing, Jesus filled his sainted tomb,
From his spirit's toil retreating, while he broke man's fatal doom;
'Twas a new creation bursting, brighter than the primal one,—
'Tis fulfilment,—reconcilement,—'tis redemption,—it is done.

Da Costa.

EVENING PRAYER AT A GIRL'S SCHOOL

> "Now in thy youth, beseech of Him,
> Who giveth, upbraiding not;
> That his light in thy heart become not dim,
> And his love be unforgot;
> And thy God, in the darkest of days, will be,
> Greenness, and beauty, and strength to thee."
> BERNARD BARTON.

HUSH! 'tis a holy hour—the quiet room
   Seems like a temple, while yon soft lamp sheds
A faint and starry radiance, through the gloom
   And the sweet stillness, down on fair young heads,
With all their clustering locks, untouched by care,
And bowed, as flowers are bowed with night, in prayer.

Gaze on—'tis lovely!—Childhood's lip and cheek,
   Mantling beneath its earnest brow of thought—
Gaze—yet what seest thou in those fair, and meek,
   And fragile things, as but for sunshine wrought?
Thou seest what grief must nurture for the sky,
What death must fashion for eternity!

O! joyous creature! that will sink to rest!
  Lightly when those pure orisons are done,
As birds with slumber's honey-dew opprest,
  'Midst the dim folded leaves, at set of sun—
Lift up your hearts! though yet no sorrow lies
Dark in the summer-heaven of those clear eyes.

Though fresh within your breasts th' untroubled
      springs
  Of hope make melody where'er ye tread,
And o'er your sleep bright shadows, from the wings
  Of spirits visiting but youth, be spread;
Yet in those flute-like voices, mingling low,
Is woman's tenderness—how soon her woe!

Her lot is on you—silent tears to weep
  And patient smiles to wear through suffering's
      hour,
And sumless riches, from affection's deep,
  To pour on broken reeds—a wasted shower!
And to make idols, and to find them clay,
And to bewail that worship—therefore pray!

Her lot is on you—to be found untired,
  Watching the stars out by the bed of pain,

With a pale cheek, and yet a brow inspired,
   And a true heart of hope, though hope be vain;
Meekly to bear with wrong, to cheer decay,
And oh! to love through all things—therefore pray!

And take the thought of this calm vesper time,
   With its low murmuring sounds and silvery light,
On through the dark days fading from their prime,
   As a sweet dew to keep your souls from blight!
Earth will forsake—O! happy to have given
Th' unbroken heart's first fragrance unto Heaven.
HEMANS.

THE GERMAN NIGHT-WATCHMAN'S SONG.

  HARK, while I sing! our village clock
  The hour of *Eight*, good Sirs, has struck.
  Eight souls alone from death were kept,
  When God the earth with deluge swept:
  Unless the Lord to guard us deign,
  Man wakes and watches all in vain.
    Lord! through thine all-prevailing might,
    Do thou vouchsafe us a good night!

Hark, while I sing! our village clock
The hour of *Nine*, good Sirs, has struck.
Nine lepers cleansed returned not;—
Be not thy blessings, man, forgot!
Unless the Lord to guard us deign,
Man wakes and watches all in vain.
 Lord! through thine all-prevailing might,
 Do thou vouchsafe us a good night!

Hark, while I sing! our village clock
The hour of *Ten*, good Sirs, has struck.
Ten precepts show God's holy will;—
O, may we prove obedient still!
Unless the Lord to guard us deign,
Man wakes and watches all in vain.
 Lord! through thine all-prevailing might,
 Do thou vouchsafe us a good night!

Hark, while I sing! our village clock
The hour *Eleven*, good Sirs, has struck.
Eleven apostles remained true;—
May we be like that faithful few!
Unless the Lord to guard us deign,
Man wakes and watches all in vain.

THE GERMAN NIGHT-WATCHMAN.

    Lord! through thine all-prevailing might,
    Do thou vouchsafe us a good night!

Hark, while I sing! our village clock
The hour of *Twelve,* good Sirs, has struck.
Twelve is of Time the boundary;—
Man, think upon Eternity!
Unless the Lord to guard us deign,
Man wakes and watches all in vain.
    Lord! through thine all-prevailing might,
    Do thou vouchsafe us a good night!

Hark, while I sing! our village clock
The hour of *One,* good Sirs, has struck.
One God alone reigns over all;
Nought can without his will befall:
Unless the Lord to guard us deign,
Man wakes and watches all in vain.
    Lord! through thine all-prevailing might,
    Do thou vouchsafe us a good night!

Hark, while I sing! our village clock
The hour of *Two,* good Sirs, has struck.
Two ways to walk has man been given;
Teach me the right,—the path to heaven!

THE GERMAN NIGHT-WATCHMAN.

Unless the Lord to guard us deign,
Man wakes and watches all in vain.
   Lord! through thine all prevailing might,
   Do thou vouchsafe us a good night!

Hark, while I sing! our village clock
The hour of *Three*, good Sirs, has struck.
Three Gods in one, exalted most,
The Father, Son, and Holy Ghost.
Unless the Lord to guard us deign,
Man wakes and watches all in vain.
   Lord! through thine all-prevailing might,
   Do thou vouchsafe us a good night!

Hark, while I sing! our village clock
The hour of *Four*, good Sirs, has struck.
Four seasons crown the farmer's care;—
Thy heart with equal toil prepare!
Up, up! awake, nor slumber on!
The morn approaches, night is gone!
   Thank God, who by his power and might
   Has watched and kept us through his night!

ANON.

CHURCH MUSIC.

SWEETEST of sweets, I thank you: when displeasure
   Did through my body wound my mind,
You took me thence, and in your house of pleasure
   A dainty lodging me assigned.

Now I in you without a body move,
   Rising and falling with your wings:
We both together sweetly live and love,
   Yet say sometimes, God help poor kings!

Comfort, I'll die; for if you post from me,
   Sure I shall do so, and much more;
But if I travel in your company,
   You know the way to heaven's door.

HERBERT.

ON OPENING A PLACE FOR SOCIAL PRAYER.

Jesus! where'er thy people meet,
There they behold thy mercy-seat:
Where'er they seek thee, thou art found,
And every place is hallowed ground.

For thou, within no walls confined,
Inhabitest the humble mind;
Such ever bring thee where they come,
And going, take thee to their home.

Dear Shepherd of thy chosen few!
Thy former mercies here renew;
Here to our waiting hearts proclaim
The sweetness of thy saving name.

Here may we prove the power of prayer,
To strengthen faith, and sweeten care;
To teach our faint desires to rise,
And bring all heaven before our eyes.

Behold, at thy commanding word
We stretch the curtain and the cord;[1]
Come thou, and fill this wider space,
And bless us with a large increase.

Lord, we are few, but thou art near;
Nor short thine arm, nor deaf thine ear;
Oh rend the heavens, come quickly down,
And make a thousand hearts thine own.

COWPER.

[1] Isaiah 64: 2.

PRAISE.

King of glory, King of peace,
    I will love thee
And, that love may never cease,
    I will move thee.

Thou hast granted my request;
    Thou hast heard me:
Thou didst note my working breast;
    Thou hast spared me.

Wherefore with my utmost art
    I will sing thee,
And the cream of all my heart
    I will bring thee.

Though my sins against me cried,
    Thou didst clear me;
And alone, when they replied,
    Thou didst hear me.

Seven whole days, not one in seven,
    I will praise thee:
In my heart, though not in heaven,
    I can raise thee.

Thou grew'st soft and moist with tears,
    Thou relentedst;
And, when Justice called for fears,
    Thou dissentedst.

Small it is, in this poor sort
    To enrol thee:
Even eternity is too short
    To extol thee
HERBERT.

THE END.

www.ingramcontent.com/pod-product-compliance
Lightning Source LLC
Chambersburg PA
CBHW031346160426
43196CB00007B/747